BE YOUR OWN

ROCK & MINERAL EXPERT

Michèle Pinet & Alain Korkos

Sterling Publishing Co., Inc.

New York

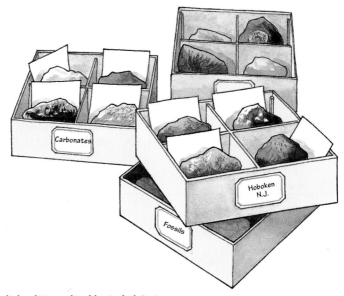

Text by Michèle Pinet
Illustrations by Alain Korkos
Translated by Fay Greenbaum; English edition edited by Isabel Stein

Library of Congress Cataloging-in-Publication Data
Pinet, Michèle.
    [Découvre les roches et les minéraux. English]
    Be your own rock & mineral expert / Michèle Pinet ;
illustrated by Alain Korkos ; [translated by Fay
Greenbaum].
        p.   cm.
    Includes index.
    Summary: Surveys various kinds of rocks and
minerals and describes how to take samples and set up
a laboratory at home.
    ISBN 0-8069-9580-7
    1. Minerals—Juvenile literature.Rocks—Juvenile
literature. [1. Rocks.2. Minerals.] I. Korkos, Alain, ill.
II. Title.
QE365.2.P5613 1997
552—dc20   96–27611
                                      CIP
                                      AC

10 9 8 7 6 5 4 3 2 1

Published 1997 by Sterling Publishing Company, Inc.
387 Park Avenue South, New York, N.Y. 10016
Originally published and © 1996 in France by Éditions
Mango under the title *Découvre les roches et les minéraux*
English translation © 1997 by Sterling Publishing Co., Inc.
Distributed in Canada by Sterling Publishing
C/o Canadian Manda Group, One Atlantic Avenue, Suite 105
Toronto, Ontario, Canada M6K 3E7
Printed in Hong Kong
All rights reserved

Sterling ISBN 0-8069-9580-7

CONTENTS

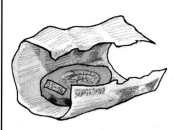

DISCOVER MINERALOGY

Whether you live in the city, the country, the mountains, or at the seashore, minerals are all around you. They are in the stones of the walls of your house and the slate of your roof, in the curbs of sidewalks, in the gravel and rocks in the road, in the earth of your garden, in the sand and pebbles of the beach. They are part of your daily life and have a long, fascinating history.

FROM PREHISTORIC TIMES TO OUR TIMES

People have been using the rocks and minerals around them for a very long time. Today, we change and adapt these basic materials to meet our needs.

Clays are formed from tiny particles of weathered rocks. Dried in the sun or baked in ovens, they become pottery, bricks, and tiles.

Arrowheads are made of flint.

Sandstones are made into bowls and pestles and used to grind grain.

Melted sand is the main component of glass windows and bottles (see p. 15).

Aluminum, a metal extracted from an ore, is laminated to plastic to form the material in fire-fighters' silver suits.

The silicon in computer chips is extracted from sand.

ROCKS, MINERALS, AND FOSSILS

A rock is made up of one or more minerals.

A mineral is a naturally occurring crystalline element or compound from the Earth's crust. Every mineral has its own chemical composition.

A fossil is the preserved remains or imprint of a plant or animal (see pp. 24–25).

quartz

mica

feldspar

Granite is an igneous rock composed of several minerals.

fossil of a fern

7

A WORLD OF MINERALS

The rocks of our planet Earth are made up of about 2500 different minerals. Rocks seem unchanging because our lives are not long enough for us to see the continual changes in the landscape. But if you had lived millions of years ago, you could have seen the pushing up of the Alps, the Pyrenees, or the Appalachian Mountains, the opening of the Red Sea, or impressive volcanic eruptions.

WHAT'S INSIDE THE EARTH?

The ocean floor, which covers 70% of the surface of the Earth, is covered in basalt. This volcanic rock comes out of the great cracks — the oceanic ridges— that furrow the oceans over more than 37 280 mi (60 000 km).

The continents are formed mostly of igneous rocks. Metamorphic and sedimentary rocks are much less important (see pp. 10–11).

THE COSMIC YEAR

This calendar shows the moment when humans appeared on Earth, compared to the history of the Universe and the Earth.

DECEMBER 28: FLOWERING PLANTS APPEAR

DECEMBER 31 10:30 P.M. FIRST HUMANS APPEAR

DECEMBER 31 11:59:59 P.M. THE MIDDLE AGES

JANUARY 1: BIRTH OF THE UNIVERSE

EARLY SEPT.: FORMATION OF THE EARTH

OCTOBER 15: LIFE APPEARS ON THE EARTH

DECEMBER 24: DINOSAURS APPEAR

J. F. M. A. M. J. J. A. S. O. N. D.

1 year on this calendar represents 15 billion (15 000 000 000) years

The Moon, our satellite, is made of rocks, as are the planets Mars, Venus, and Mercury, and also the meteorites.

Below the crust, the Earth's mantle is made up of hot, dense, crystalline rocks, that are slowly moving. Of the rocks we commonly find at the surface of the Earth, geologic processes have brought rocks from only 150 miles (250 km) in the mantle to the surface. They are peridotites.

The deepest drilling is on the Kola Peninsula in Russia: it reaches 8 miles (13 km), while the radius of the Earth is 3975 miles (6,370 km).

Thanks to the study of the vibrations from earthquakes, scientists were able to establish that our planet is made of successive spherical shells around a core.

The outer core is made of liquid iron and nickel.

The Earth's crust is a relatively thin layer on the surface of the globe. It is thicker under mountains (43½ miles or 70 km) than in the plains (18½ miles or 30 km) or at the bottom of the ocean, where it is 6.2 miles (10 km).

The inner core is, without a doubt, solid. It is made up of almost pure iron, with a little nickel. At the center of the Earth, temperatures can reach 9000°F (5000°C).

THE EARTH'S CRUST IS VERY THIN

In order to understand, take a thread 21 feet (6.4 m) long and attach it to a stake, which will represent the center of the Earth. Pull the thread taut and draw a circle. Now, measure 1 inch (3 cm) in from the end you are holding in your hand. Make another circle starting from this new mark. The thin ring around the outside of the circle between the two lines represents the crust. You can get an idea of the relative thicknesses of the mantle and the core by drawing a new circle 11.4 feet (3.5 m) out from the stake (see illustration).

ONE SECOND LATER, WORLD OF TODAY

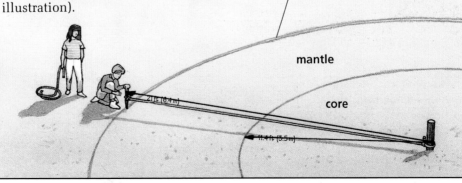

Earth's crust

mantle

core

21 ft (6.4 m)

11.4 ft (3.5 m)

SEDIMENTARY ROCKS

Some sedimentary rocks come from the accumulation of the debris of other rocks.

Conglomerates are deposits of rounded pebbles of various rocks and sand grains united by a natural cement.

It sometimes takes millions of years for sediments to be transformed into rock.

Sandstone is sand that has become cemented together.

Other sedimentary rocks are formed by the accumulation of calcium- or silica-containing shells of tiny organisms.

Chalk is a soft limestone made up of tens of millions of coccoliths (the remains of tiny sea organisms).

If you are looking for fossils (see pp. 24–25), you will find most of them in sedimentary rocks, particularly in limestone.

The evaporation of seawater gives us evaporites, sedimentary rocks such as gypsum.

rock salt   seawater evaporation
                   pond in a salt marsh

The sea is salty because the continual erosion of rocks brings it salts, which remain dissolved in the water.

Oil and carbon are sedimentary deposits made from the accumulation and the transformation of the remains of plants, algae, and various other organisms.

drilling platform for oil in the sea

carbon

METAMORPHIC ROCKS

In the depths of the Earth, sedimentary and igneous rocks are subjected to great pressures as well as very high temperatures. Under these conditions, the original minerals are no longer stable and the rocks change in nature. For example, limestone becomes marble. The marble is colored and veined in various colors if the original limestone has impurities. Clay may become slate, schist, phyllite, or several other rocks.

Marble is one of the materials that has been preferred for thousands of years by sculptors.

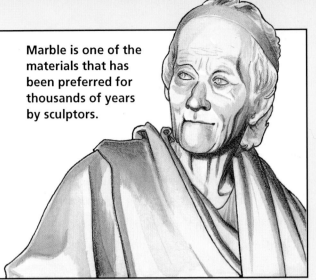

IGNEOUS ROCKS

Igneous rocks also come from the depths of the Earth, where they are magmas whose temperatures are greater than 1800°F (1000°C; see pp. 8–9).

If the cooling of the magma is slow (if it remains deep in the Earth, for example), plutonic rocks are formed.

If the cooling is rapid, as in volcanic eruptions, volcanic rock (lava) is formed.

Granite is a plutonic rock.

A ROCK THAT FLOATS

Get a piece of natural pumice; put it in a basin. What do you notice? Pumice is the only rock that floats in water; in fact, this volcanic rock contains many small, enclosed spaces, which have no contact with the outside. This makes it less dense than water, so it floats.

Obsidian, a volcanic rock, is a glass made when lava cools very rapidly and there is no time for crystals to form. Obsidian ranges in color from dark green to black.

Basalt is a black volcanic rock that sometimes contains crystals of a green mineral, olivine.

A FIELD TRIP

Now that you have learned to recognize several rocks, go out and explore the landscape in your area. To do this, you must prepare for your trip. Don't take too much gear; a bag filled with samples is heavy enough to carry back at the end of the day.

MAKE YOUR OWN CLINOMETER

A clinometer is used to measure the incline of a piece of land. Find the middle of one of the two long sides of a board. Make a small mark and place the center of a protractor on that spot.

protractor

wooden board
6 in × 3 in × ½ in
(15 × 7.5 × 1 cm)

Draw a semicircle along the outer edge of the protractor and transfer the angles from 0 to 90°, reversing them from the way they are marked on the protractor: 0° should be at the bottom center.

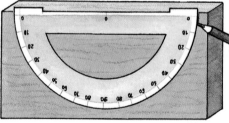

Remove the protractor and hammer in a nail at the small mark at the center of the semicircle.

Make a loop at one end of a thin metal rod (such as part of a paper clip) and place this loop around the nail. The rod should not go past the base.

round-headed nail
2½ inches long
(6 cm)

Measure the angle of a book leaning up against some others. For land, this angle is called the angle of dip.

thin
metal
rod

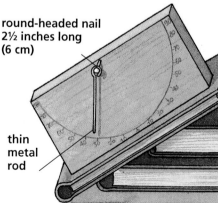

a pair of goggles to protect you from chips flying off the rocks you break

a pad for writing down things you notice about the terrain and for making a list of your samples (see p. 20)

The samples you find will depend on where you are: seaside, mountains, plains....

The geological survey map of your area will be useful in orienting you, and also in helping you make a survey of the area (see p. 20).

SAFETY MEASURES

1. Always alert people from your group of the route you plan to take, and don't change it.
2. Never go alone.
3. Never follow railroad tracks; in most places it is illegal and it always is extremely dangerous.
4. Wear a safety helmet if you are walking under a cliff.
5. Ask for permission when going onto private property or into quarries.
6. Turn over stones cautiously, as you can disturb sleeping snakes or other reptiles.

Leather gloves protect your hands from badly placed hammer blows when you collect your samples.

Don't forget that it can rain, be cold, and you can get hungry or thirsty....

walking shoes

If your compass does not have a clinometer, make one (see the opposite page).

a roll of adhesive tape to number your samples (see p. 19)

chisel

This geologist's hammer lets you take samples and make fresh breaks in rocks. What's more, its length can serve as a measuring rod if you take photos of rocks in the field.

AT THE SEASHORE

Each year, erosion removes more than 24 billion (24 000 000 000) tons of solids and dissolved materials from the surface of the continents; eventually they reach the sea. Landslides, slowly advancing glaciers, and streaming waters in brooks and rivers carry these materials toward the sea.

As you get closer to the sea, you notice the sand becoming finer; in effect, the grains of quartz have been worn down more by the sea. The action of the waves also wears down seashells.

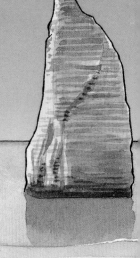

Pebbles form borders at the upper ends of beaches.

PEBBLE EXPERT

High water and storms break off pieces of rock from the cliffs, which, endlessly rolled by the movement of the waves, are progressively worn down to create pebbles. The shape of the pebbles depends on the nature and hardness of the minerals in the cliff.

Ovoid pebbles are made of sandstone, quartzite, flint....

A group of pebbles glued together with natural cement is a pudding stone.

Disk-shaped pebbles often are of limestone, shale, schist, or mica schist.

Rounded ones are made of granite.

SAND EXPERT

Water and wind both transport sand, but they do not wear it down in the same way. Study the shape and look of sand grains from different places to learn to identify them.

Grains of river sand can be of any shape, and have sharp edges, as they have been subjected to only slight movement.

Grains of sand from the seashore are egg-shaped, with a shiny surface; the ebb and flow of the sea has worn and polished the grains for a long time.

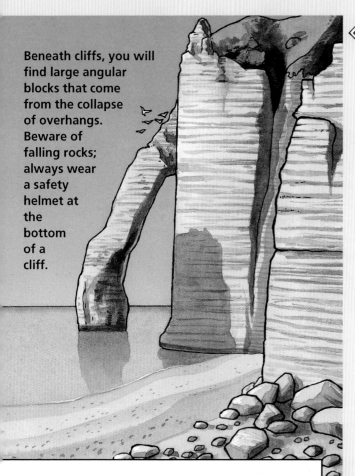

Beneath cliffs, you will find large angular blocks that come from the collapse of overhangs. Beware of falling rocks; always wear a safety helmet at the bottom of a cliff.

The joining of grains of sand makes sandstone.

Grains of desert sand are rounded and are covered with grooves and the traces of their hitting against one another. This gives them a matte finish. Wind wear is harsher than wear by water.

TRAVELS OF A SAND GRAIN

Changes in rocks free grains of quartz, feldspar, mica.... Some grains, softer than quartz, are weathered and disappear. The slowing down of the current along the length of a river favors the depositing of sand.

On arriving at the sea, the grains are dispersed by ocean currents... a beach is formed.

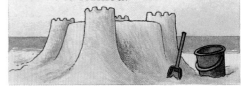

This is why you can find grains of sand on the beaches that came from far up in the mountains.

SAND AND GLASS

Sand made of grains of quartz is used in the manufacture of glass. Mixed with other substances and heated to 2642° F (1450° C), it yields a glass paste, which is then shaped.

The sand for glass-making must be very pure. Less than 1% iron oxide will discolor glass and make it unusable for windows.

IN THE COUNTRY

Forests and cultivated areas often hide rocks. However, if you are observant, you can easily tell what kinds of rocks can be found underneath. Study the stones of the houses and churches in the area; they are often built of native materials.

In volcanic regions, basalt blocks are used in the walls of houses.

CLASSIFYING GRAINS OF SAND

Mix water and river sand in a bottle. Shake well; then let it sit for several days.

The layers will be deposited according to the size of the grains; the largest reach the bottom first.

With beach sand, a single layer forms, because the grains all are more or less the same size.

Natural outcroppings of rock are rare; so take advantage of road building or construction work to observe rocks in place.

In sedimentary regions, limestones are easily cut (freestone) and are easily sculpted. Buhrstone and sandstone are also used.

In metamorphic regions, schists and mica schists are used. Roofs often are made of slate.

Look at the low walls; they frequently are built with stones taken from the fields.

16

IN THE CITY

The city is an excellent place to study, as it brings together many kinds of rocks and even fossils, although you can't remove them.

Today, houses are built from prefabricated elements, such as bricks and tiles, or ones prepared on the spot, like concrete. Their manufacture requires naturally occurring minerals and rocks: clay, gravel, sand, and limestone for cement; and gypsum for plaster.

Visit museums of natural history; you can ask for information from specialists.

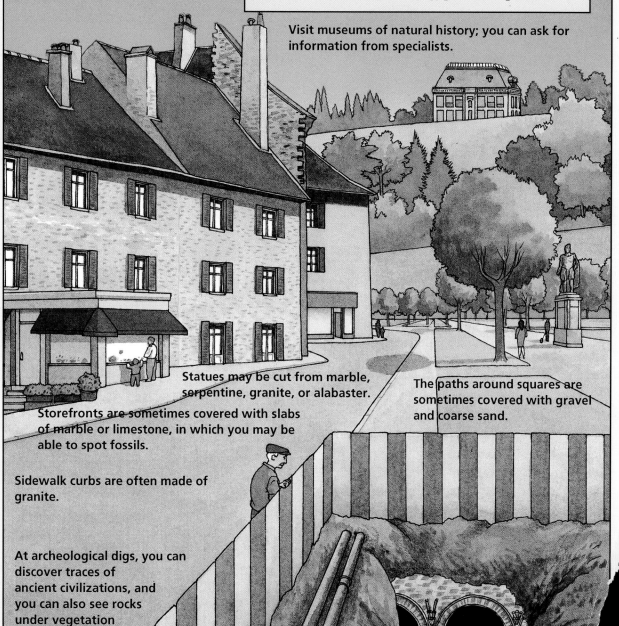

Statues may be cut from marble, serpentine, granite, or alabaster.

The paths around squares are sometimes covered with gravel and coarse sand.

Storefronts are sometimes covered with slabs of marble or limestone, in which you may be able to spot fossils.

Sidewalk curbs are often made of granite.

At archeological digs, you can discover traces of ancient civilizations, and you can also see rocks under vegetation there.

17

VOLCANOS

In an area where there are old volcanos (like Sunset Crater, Arizona, and Mt. Shasta, California), you can collect solid fragments of lava called tephra, which sometimes pile up on the sides of the volcano.

Small pieces less than 2 mm in diameter are called ash. Lapilli are small fragments (2 to 64 mm). Bombs (more than 64 mm) can weigh several kilograms; their surface is fused or crusted like bread.

Lava rocks that are not very viscous, like the basalts, show horizontal stacking of flows.

basalt

peridotite nodule

Certain lava rocks dragged along fragments of rocks such as peridotites, rich in olivine, from the Earth's upper mantle, as they rose up.

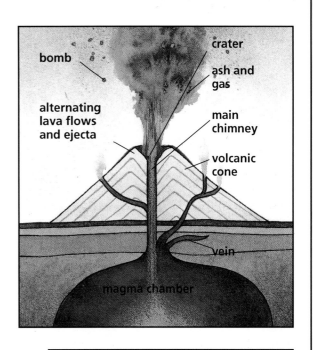

bomb

crater

ash and gas

alternating lava flows and ejecta

main chimney

volcanic cone

vein

magma chamber

DID YOU KNOW?

Because lava rocks crystallize rapidly, the crystals that they are made up of are small.

IN THE MOUNTAINS

Past the tree line, rocks are bare and you can collect many samples.
In the mountains you can most easily see the tectonics of rocks: study the folds, breaks or faults, and stratification.

GEOLOGIST'S ENVELOPES

In order to carry small fossils or sand, geologists use tubes or make envelopes with a quarter sheet of 8½ × 11 inch (21.5 × 28 cm) paper.

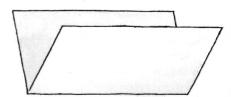

1. Fold the sheet in half lengthwise.

TAKING SAMPLES

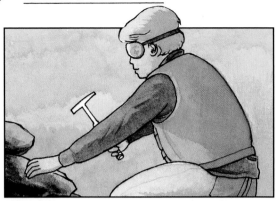

Break a rock that is in place; do not gather it from a rock slide (rock slides can come from different rocks, which were brought by erosion). Hit the hammer on a rock point to break off a fragment. The fresh break will enable you to better observe the organization and size of the minerals combined in the rock. If the minerals are small, use a

magnifying glass. Number your samples and write the number in indelible ink on a piece of adhesive tape, and stick it on your sample, avoiding damp areas, so that it will stay on well. Copy the sample's location number onto your map (see p. 20).

In order to avoid breaking a fossil, take some of the surrounding rock with it; you will have time to free it from the rock at home.

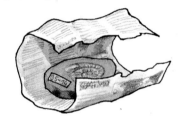

Wrap your sample in newspaper and put it in your backpack.

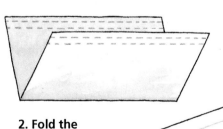

2. Fold the edges over on themselves two times; each fold is about ¼ inch (5 mm) wide.

3. Fold down the upper corners as shown.

4. Fold the points upward; tuck each under the edge fold.

A LAND SURVEY

To make a geological survey, all you have to do is look carefully at the countryside as you walk around.

Plan your trip by circling an area (one that is not too large) on a survey map. This map can be the basis of your topographical map; you will write on it your observations about the kind of rocks you notice (such as limestone, sandstone, clay, schist, granite), and the direction (strike) and the angle of dip of the strata (see p. 21).

To make a land survey, follow the roads and paths that are indicated on your map. Every time you notice a change in the rocks (for example, sandstone becomes limestone), mark the boundary of these two kinds of rocks with a line on your map; continue in this way along all the roads you survey.

Gradually, you will cover the terrain of interest to you.

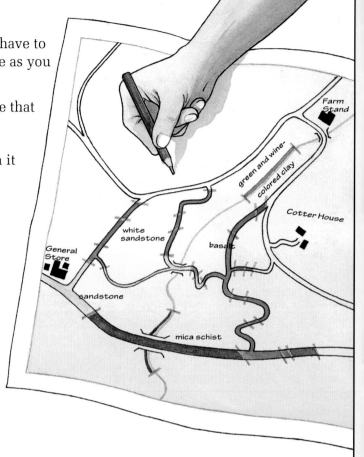

YOUR FIELD NOTEBOOK

To avoid overloading your map, write your observations about rocks in your field notebook. For example:
– the color of the rocks: grey, white, yellowish
–the grain of the rocks: coarse, medium, fine
–the shape of the rocks: in beds, slabs, blocks, layers
The shape depends on the succession of layers of varying graininess. For example, in sandstone, layers of medium grain may alternate with very fine-grained layers.

*Inwood Hill Park
–The entire length of the highway: grey rocks, medium grain, boulders*

THE DIP AND DIRECTION OF STRATA

In order to understand what the dip and direction (strike) of a piece of land are, do the following experiment.

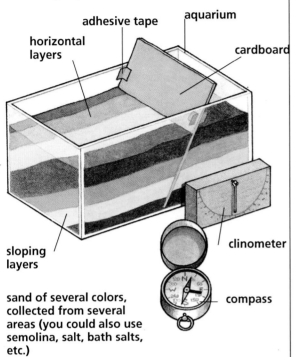

adhesive tape

aquarium

horizontal layers

cardboard

sloping layers

clinometer

compass

sand of several colors, collected from several areas (you could also use semolina, salt, bath salts, etc.)

Using adhesive tape, firmly fix a piece of cardboard at an angle in an empty aquarium. Pour in layers of sand in different colors as shown in the picture. Even out the sand on the surface.

Measure the angle of dip of a layer.

The dip is the slope of your layer, the angle it forms with the horizontal.

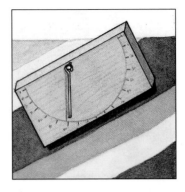

Place your clinometer against the outside of the aquarium, tilting it so that it follows the slope of one of the layers of sand.

Measure the strike of a layer. This is the angle your layer forms with magnetic north.

Place your compass on the surface of the sand in the aquarium. Its needle will point to magnetic north. Measure the angle one of the layers makes with magnetic north.

The angle of dip and the direction (strike) enable geologists to know how layers are positioned underground.

MINES AND QUARRIES

In mines, tunnels are dug following a seam or a layer as closely as possible, in order to dig out minerals. In quarries, the layers are uncovered. Find out if your area has mines or quarries; always visit them with an adult.

CAUTION

–Never enter the tunnel of an abandoned mine.
–A quarry is a dangerous place; don't go there without permission.

YOUR MINERALOGICAL LABORATORY

When you get home, you will be able to study the samples you've brought back. You will have to remove and classify your fossils and identify your rocks and their minerals. You can also use your observations in the field to draw a geological map.

IDENTIFYING A ROCK

Recognizing a specific mineral may be difficult, but certain signs will enable you to recognize the big groups.

Sedimentary rocks: The presence of fossils indicates that you have a sedimentary rock.
They are often formed from deposits of a single mineral (calcite for limestone; quartz for sandstone).
Clay sticks to the tongue and breaks easily in your hand.

Volcanic (extrusive igneous) rocks: Crystals are not visible to the naked eye; they formed quickly from cooled lava. The rocks usually are grey, black, or dark green, and the color is uniform. Obsidians are glassy.

Plutonic (intrusive igneous) rocks: The component minerals (for example, quartz, feldspar, mica in granite) are visible to the naked eye. They formed from magma that cooled slowly underground.

Metamorphic rocks: These have the same minerals as igneous rocks, but they are distributed in layers (like a pastry) and are often folded. The layers are all alike and can be split (like slate), or they alternate (like mica schist).

CALCULATING THE SPECIFIC GRAVITY OF YOUR ROCKS

The specific gravity of a rock is the ratio of the weight of a rock to the weight of an equal volume of water. Measuring the specific gravity of your samples will help you identify them, as each mineral has a characteristic specific gravity.

MATERIALS

kitchen scale   small container   lightweight bowl

1. Weigh your rock *(x)*.
2. Weigh your bowl.
3. Put your small container in the bowl and fill the small container to the brim with water.

4. Gently lower your sample into the water.

5. The water overflows into the bowl; the water in the bowl has the same volume as your sample.

22

YOUR GEOLOGICAL MAP

Take out the map you made in your land survey (see p. 20). Join the borders between your rock observation lines by stippling; you will see areas corresponding to each kind of rock emerge in your drawing. If you color them in, they will look even better to you.

Compare your geological map with one made by geologists for the same area; in this way you can check your work and complete it.

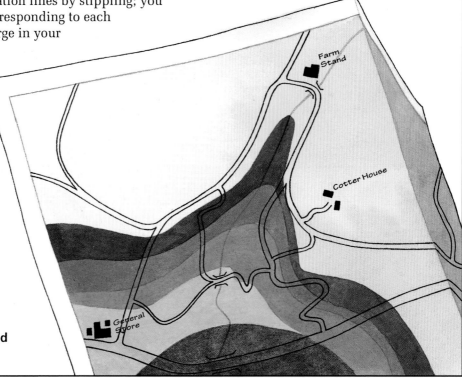

6. Remove the small container holding the water and the rock, taking care not to spill any more water into the bowl.
7. Weigh the bowl plus the overflow water *(z)*.

8. Calculate the weight of the water *p*
$$z - y = p$$
The specific gravity *(d)* of your rock is the weight of the rock *(x)* divided by the weight of the water *(p)*.

Weight of the rock: 54 g = x
Weight of the bowl: 180 g = y
Weight of the bowl plus the overflowed water: 200 g = z
Weight of the water $(p) = 20$ g
because 200 g – 180 g = 20 g
Specific gravity of the rock (d)
= $x / p = 54 / 20 = 2.7$

As the specific gravity of water equals 1, any object with a greater specific gravity will sink; an object will float if its specific gravity is less than 1. Pumice stone is the only stone that floats in water (see p. 11).

FOSSILS

In theory, many plants and animals could have become fossils, but few found favorable enough conditions to do so. Only organisms quickly buried in the sediment of lakes or oceans, caught in ice, or stuck in tar or plant resin have left a fossil record.

The animal in its natural habitat

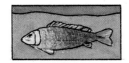

The dead animal is soon buried in sediment.

The skeleton, covered in sediment, is preserved and compressed.

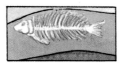

The skeleton is revealed by erosion

MAKING A CAST OF YOUR FOSSIL

Brush your fossil with several layers of flexible moldmaking compound (sold in hobby shops for model making); then let it dry well. With a hobby knife, carefully cut open the resulting mold and remove your fossil. Fill the mold with plaster of paris to make a replica of your fossil. Remove it when dry and paint if desired.

REMOVING THE FOSSIL

Start by attaching the rock enclosing your fossil to a thick board fitted with blocks to keep the specimen from moving.

Look at the surface of your sample under a magnifying glass; it may contain plant or animal parts.

4. Always hammer in a direction away from the fossil in order to avoid damaging it.

1. With wood glue and nails, attach two strips of wood to a board.

2. Nail on two other small, moveable blocks to hold your rock and a third block to hold a rotatable magnifying glass.

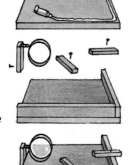

3. Little by little, using a small chisel and a light hammer, carefully chip away the surrounding rock. Protect your eyes with goggles.

IDENTIFYING YOUR FOSSIL

Identifying the species of your fossil without the help of a specialist is not an easy task. On the other hand, you can discover what large group it belongs to with the help of photos and drawings, which you can find in books on the natural sciences and paleontology.

It will be easy for you to identify fossils whose shapes are fairly close to present-day animals or plants.

Some fossils have very few living relatives; some have none.

corals

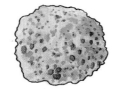

sponges

Brachiopods have two unequal shells, which are smooth or have growth lines.

gastropods (snails)

Ammonites have shells that often have decorative-looking lobelines.

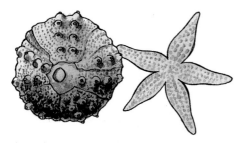

echinoderms (sea urchins and starfish)

Belemnites resemble today's cuttlefish and squid. Only their strange internal shells, shaped liked rifle bullets, are usually found.

lamellibranches (cockles, mussels, scallops)

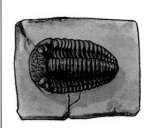

Trilobites have no living relatives. Their bodies, made up of a head, a three-lobed rump, and a tail plate, were able to curl up like those of wood lice.

IDENTIFYING MINERALS

Rocks are formed from one or more minerals. Look in the cracks of rocks, as they are often lined with small crystals, which you can study. Break your rock samples and sort out each mineral grain from the powder you get, with the help of a magnifying glass. Several tests of the physical characteristics of minerals will help you to identify them.

Is the mineral soluble in water?

Rock salt dissolves in water.

Quartz does not dissolve in water.

Luster: certain minerals reflect light well.

Pyrites have a metallic luster.

Quartz is a glassy mineral with very little luster.

The color of a mineral when crushed can be different from its color in crystal form. For example, pyrite (yellow) leaves black streaks. Rub your mineral on unglazed white porcelain; it attracts the powder of the streak.

Some minerals have a flavor. Rock salt (halite) is salty; sulfates have a metallic taste (geologists call this "astringent"). But most minerals have no flavor.

Transparency is the quality of letting light through.

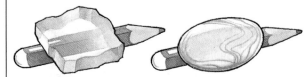

Quartz may be transparent like a pane of glass.

Opal is translucent (only diffused light passes through).

A mineral's hardness is its resistance to being scratched. In order to discover it, make your own hardness scale (see box opposite).

To estimate your sample's hardness, try to scratch it with other minerals, starting with the softest.

yellow pyrite leaves a black streak

lodestone leaves a black streak

hematite leaves a red streak

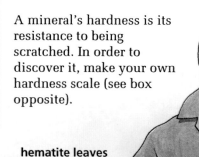

Cleavage is the property of some minerals to break in characteristic directions, which is a reflection of their internal structure.

Break a crystal of galena: you will get small cubes, which, broken again, will give you more cubes.

Break off flakes of mica by pushing the blade of a penknife into its edge.

It is not possible to cleave some minerals; they break irregularly. Quartz is an example.

MAKING A HARDNESS SCALE

The standard hardness scale, invented by Friedrich Mohs, consists of ten levels, each one represented by a mineral; you can use an equivalent object (an iron nail for level 4, for example). A mineral with a higher number can scratch those whose numbers are lower than it. In this way, you can learn the hardness of an unknown mineral, a clue to identification.

Hardness	Test mineral	Possible equivalents
1	talc	kaolin, graphite (lead of a soft pencil)
2	gypsum	rock salt, fingernail (2.2)
3	calcite	bronze (3.5), copper coin (3)
4	fluorite	iron nail
5	apatite	glass (5.5), knife blade
6	orthoclase	hard steel, steel file (6.5)
7	quartz	agate
8	topaz	sandpaper
9	corundum	emery paper
10	diamond	(no equivalent)

Gather minerals or their equivalents for the first 9 levels of hardness. Arrange them and label them. Do your tests on the least attractive areas of your crystals. Brush away the powder that forms from testing so that you can see the scratches clearly.

WHAT IS A CRYSTAL?

Most minerals are made up of crystals, solid bodies with regularly repeating geometric shapes. Each mineral has a precise chemical composition, which results from the number, kind, and position of its atoms. In crystals, atoms are grouped in patterns which repeat regularly, forming a kind of lattice. There are seven types of lattice: the seven crystal systems.

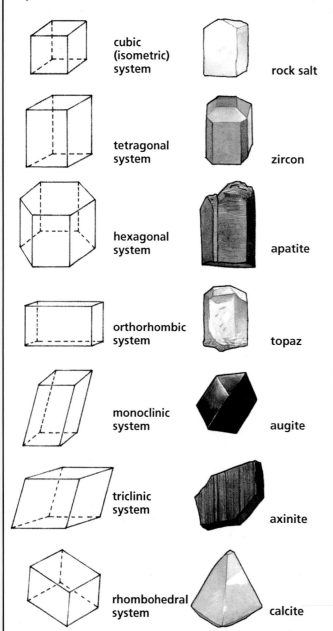

cubic (isometric) system

rock salt

tetragonal system

zircon

hexagonal system

apatite

orthorhombic system

topaz

monoclinic system

augite

triclinic system

axinite

rhombohedral system

calcite

LOOKING AT SNOWFLAKES

Snowflakes are hexagonal crystals. If you let a few flakes rest on a black cloth and look at them with a magnifying glass, you can see that their shapes are very varied, but they always form hexagons if you measure along the outside points.

THE SIZE OF CRYSTALS

The longer the conditions of their formation last, the larger crystals become. In this way, it is possible for the same mineral to yield microcrystals, invisible to the naked eye, and giant crystals, several yards (meters) long.

MAKING CRYSTALS DISAPPEAR

Crystals disappear when placed in conditions in which they are not in equilibrium; for example, some crystals when heated will change from their crystalline state. Heat sugar crystals in a saucepan. On melting, the crystals form a liquid. Put this liquid in the freezer; it will cool quickly and will become a brittle, transparent solid (it hasn't had the time to crystallize).

MAKING HALITE CRYSTALS

It is best to do this experiment in the summer, so that the water will evaporate quickly.

1. Fill a bowl with warm water and dissolve a large quantity of sea salt; your solution should be supersaturated (no more salt will dissolve).

2. Pour your solution into an empty plate.

3. Leave your plate in the sun for one day and one night. Look at it from time to time to make sure the water is evaporating.

4. You will see the first crystals forming and growing. Be patient, as crystals form slowly.

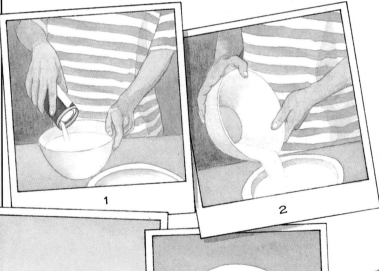

1

2

3

4

Halite (rock salt) crystals are cubic; they become rectangular solids if some sides develop more quickly than others. Several crystals can also grow into each other (interpenetrate).

UNUSUAL PROPERTIES OF CRYSTALS

Magnetism

Some minerals are magnetic — magnetite, for example. You can check this with a very simple experiment.

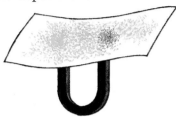

Put a little sand on a sheet of paper. Move a magnet back and forth under the sheet so that it separates the magnetic minerals from those that are not.

Effervescence

This property will be useful to you in recognizing certain carbonates.

Put several drops of vinegar (which contains acetic acid) on limestone or another carbonate; you can see bubbling, caused by the release of carbon dioxide.

Pyroelectricity and piezoelectricity

Changes in temperature or in pressure cause some minerals to become electrically charged. (*Pyr-* is the prefix meaning "heat"; *piez* means "pressure.")

Study pyro-electricity: in the dark, rub two pieces of flint together. You can see sparks.

Fluorescence and phosphorescence

When some minerals are lit by ultraviolet light (which is invisible to us), they emit visible light. When a mineral emits light while the ultraviolet light is on, it is said to be fluorescent. When a mineral emits visible light even when the ultraviolet illumination ends, it is said to be phosphorescent. Phosphorescence decreases in intensity over time.

You can enjoy the magnificent colors of fluorescent minerals by visiting collections of fluorescent minerals in museums.

LOOKING INSIDE MINERALS

Solid, liquid and gaseous inclusions

Study a transparent mineral— quartz, for example. Some areas seem transparent. Others appear cloudy, due to numerous small cavities which are empty or which enclose water in a liquid or gaseous state, carbon dioxide, crystals of rock salt, or other minerals. These inclusions can sometimes be seen with the naked eye.

In this piece of quartz, you can see other minerals, which were trapped during the crystal's formation.

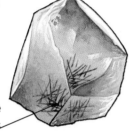

tourmaline needles

Microfractures

Microfractures, which can be found in some crystals, create iridescent areas with rainbow colors.

Refraction

Look at the surface of water as you dip a stick in it. The stick looks broken, because the speed of light is not the same in the air as it is in water. When light bouncing back from the stick hits the boundary between the two substances, it bends. The ratio of the speed of light in a vacuum to its speed in a particular substance is called the index of refraction. It is used in identifying minerals. (Refraction means *bending.*) The luster of a mineral is related to its index of refraction; the higher the index of refraction, the greater the luster.

Double refraction

Some minerals split light into 2 rays that are bent in slightly different directions. Look at a needle through a piece of transparent glass; then look at the needle through calcite. Looking through the glass, you get only a single image of the needle; through the calcite, you see two images.

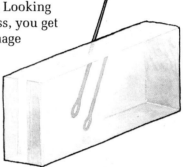

DID YOU KNOW?

Some minerals quickly turn black when exposed to light. They must be preserved with special lighting when they are collected and displayed.

The air pollution in cities attacks cathedral stones and public buildings, and also has a harmful effect on minerals in collections.

Azurite was used to make a blue pigment in old paintings. As it gradually changes into malachite, another mineral, the blue skies become greener.

CLASSIFYING SAMPLES

How should you organize your collection? Start by deciding what you want to collect. The large rock families (sedimentary, metamorphic, igneous)? Only fossils? Or maybe everything you found in a certain quarry, mine, area, or state. Learn more about your collection by reading books or magazines, by visiting museums, and by going into the field. You will be able to refine your classifications and become an expert.

LABELING YOUR SAMPLES

Sample number: 95-14
Name of mineral: Franklinite
Variety: --
Found at: Site next to Main Street
Area, town: Franklin
State: New Jersey
Country: USA

Make an index card for each of your samples, copying down its number on the card. In this way you will have a general overview of your collection and will be able to make searches quickly.

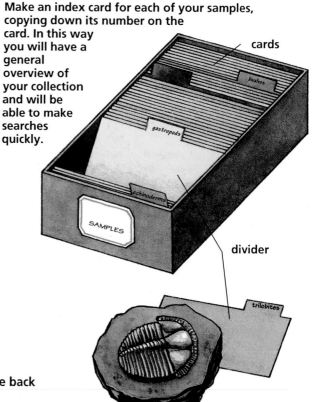

Store name: Harry's Hobbys
City: Hoboken, N.J.
Date of sale: March 31, 1997
Salesman: Murray Jones
Cost: $4.
Chemical formula: $ZnFe_2O_4$
Crystal system: cubic

Put the information about your purchase on the back of your label if you bought your sample.

ARRANGING YOUR SAMPLES

Large samples. Number your sample; here is the 14th sample found in 1995.

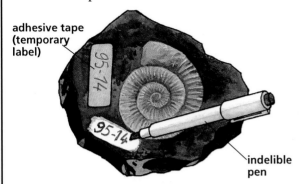

adhesive tape
(temporary
label)

indelible
pen

Paint a little rectangle of white paint on your sample; when the paint is dry, mark the inventory number with indelible ink. Then you can take the adhesive tape label off.

Put your labeled sample in a cardboard box. Cover the box with a sheet of plastic wrap or kraft paper so that dust will not get in it.

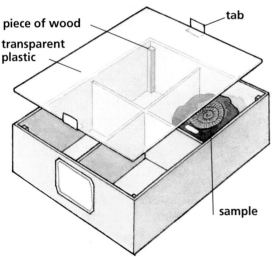

piece of wood

transparent
plastic

tab

sample

You can also protect your samples with a piece of transparent plastic. Place it on small pieces of wood glued to the corners of the box. In order to move the plastic easily, make tabs; fold two 1-inch (2 cm) pieces of cardboard in half and attach half of each to the bottom of the piece of plastic.

Micromountings

Micromountings of small objects let you display small crystals taken from a geode or from a crack in a rock, or tiny fossils.

MATERIALS

matches   small plastic boxes
modeling clay   or tubes
glue   identification labels

The cover of the box should not touch your sample when closed.

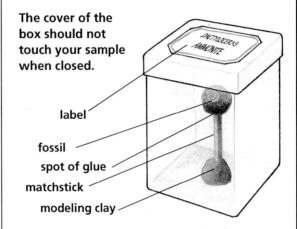

label

fossil

spot of glue

matchstick

modeling clay

With a spot of glue, attach the crystal or fossil to the uncoated end of the matchstick; keep the most interesting part of the sample facing up. Stick a piece of modeling clay to the bottom of the plastic box. Keep the match vertical while sticking it into the modeling clay.

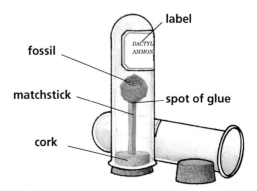

label

fossil

DACTYL
AMMON

matchstick

spot of glue

cork

GLOSSARY

Acetic acid: the main acid in vinegar; used for testing carbonates. It will cause carbonates to release carbon dioxide bubbles when applied to the rocks.

Angle of dip: slope or incline of a layer or seam, compared to the horizontal. The angle of dip is measured with a clinometer, which reads 0 when the layer is horizontal and 90° when it is vertical.

Anticline: an upfold in rock layers.

Atom: the smallest particle of an element that has all the properties of that element. Atoms of some elements can combine with one or more other elements; for example, chlorine atoms (Cl) and sodium atoms (Na) can combine to make sodium chloride, table salt (NaCl).

Azurite: this mineral, which contains copper, ranges in color from azure blue to midnight blue. It is often found with malachite in copper mines. In the US it is found in New Mexico and Arizona.

Bed: mass of rocks forming a layer of greater or lesser thickness.

Bitumen: a natural black asphalt material. Bitumen was once used to make boats watertight and as a cement or mortar.

Buhrstone: a sedimentary rock, once used to make millstones to grind grain.

Carbonate: a compound containing ion groups made up of one carbon atom combined with three oxygen atoms. Examples are: calcium carbonate, potassium carbonate, sodium carbonate.

Carbon dioxide: a colorless gas, chemical formula CO_2, produced by breathing, combustion, fermentation, and by the action of acids on carbonates.

Chalk: a soft limestone made up of tens of millions of coccoliths, the remains of tiny sea organisms.

Clay: a seafloor sediment made up of tiny flakes of material that settle to the bottom of an ocean.

Cleavage: tendency of some minerals to split easily along planes parallel to a crystal face, leaving smooth, flat surfaces in one or more directions.

Clinometer: an instrument used to measure the angle of inclination (dip) or elevation of a piece of land or other geologic structure.

Compression: pushing together of objects as the result of pressure. Over the course of geological time, rocks are subject to pressure in the Earth; the main results are the folding of mountains and metamorphosis of rocks into other rocks.

Computer chip: electronic component essential to the functioning of a computer.

Crust: layer of lighter rock that covers the Earth's mantle.

Crystals: Solid bodies with regularly repeating geometric shapes, formed by the solidification under favorable conditions of an element or compound into a regularly repeating internal arrangement of atoms called a lattice.

Density: the weight of a unit of volume of a body.

Earth's magnetic field: the Earth behaves like an enormous magnet with a South Pole and a North Pole. You can detect the Earth's magnetic field with a compass.

Effervescence: bubbling produced by the release of carbon dioxide bubbles when an acid (for example, hydrochloric acid or acetic acid) is placed on a carbonate.

Element: a substance that cannot be broken down into simpler substances by ordinary chemical or physical means. Oxygen, sodium, chlorine, and carbon are examples of elements.

Emery paper: paper covered with corundum powder; corundum is a mineral whose hardness is 9. Emery paper is used as an abrasive.

Erosion: the breakup and transport of earth materials by moving natural agents, such as wind and water.

Evaporites: sedimentary rocks formed by the evaporation of seawater in enclosed basins.

Fault: a break or crack in the Earth's crust along which movement has occurred, which may result in a difference in the level or position of the rock layers on either side of the fracture.

Flake: thin fragment of rock.

Fluorescence: property of certain minerals to emit light when illuminated by ultraviolet light or irradiated by X-rays, both of which are invisible to our eyes. When the light source is removed, the mineral no longer gives off light.

Fossil: the preserved remains or imprint of a plant or animal.

Fracture: appearance of a mineral surface that has broken along other than the cleavage planes.

Hardness: ability of one substance to scratch another. Hardness is used as a way of identifying unknown minerals as each has a characteristic hardness. A mineral's hardness depends on the arrangement of its

atoms or ions and the strength of the electric forces among them. *See also* Mohs hardness scale.

Igneous rocks: rocks that are formed by the solidification of magma, either underground (plutonic igneous rocks) or above ground (volcanic igneous rocks).

Inclusion: solid, liquid, or gaseous particles of another substance contained in a mineral or rock.

Index of refraction: ratio of the speed of light in a vacuum to its speed in a particular substance. A mineral's index of refraction is used to help identify it.

Iridescent areas: areas in a mineral in which you can see the colors of the rainbow. They are easier to see in transparent minerals.

Lava: molten rock that reaches the Earth's surface.

Luster: the shine of a mineral surface; may help to identify the mineral.

Magma: hot liquid rock beneath the Earth's surface, formed by the fusion of the Earth's crust or mantle. When magma cools down inside the Earth, it becomes plutonic rock (granite, for example). When magma rises to the surface as a liquid, it forms volcanic rock when it cools (basalt, for example).

Magnetism: property of some objects to attract metallic particles as a magnet does.

Magnetite: this mineral is an iron oxide (Fe_2O_3) that is a natural magnet.

Malachite: this green to greenish black mineral is a carbonate of hydrated copper.

Mantle: the layer of rock on the Earth that extends from its crust downward 1771 mi (2850 km).

Metamorphic rocks: rocks formed by the

effect of heat, pressure, and chemical action on other rocks in the Earth's crust.

Mica: soft silicate minerals with flat shiny flakes that are found in many rocks, such as granite and gneiss.

Mineral: a naturally occurring crystalline element or compound from the Earth's crust. Each mineral has a characteristic chemical composition and characteristic physical properties.

Mohs' hardness scale: scale for identifying minerals that was invented by Viennese mineralogist Friedrich Mohs. Hardness is defined here as the ability of the specimen to resist scratches. The scale ranges from very soft, 1 (talc), to very hard, 10 (diamond). Each mineral in the scale can scratch all the ones with lower numbers.

Obsidian: a glassy volcanic rock.

Overhang: part of a cliff which extends beyond the parts beneath it.

Ovoid: resembling an egg in shape.

Phosphorescence: property of certain minerals to emit visible light when illuminated by ultraviolet light or irradiation by X-rays, which continues for some time after the utraviolet light or X-rays are stopped. The length of time the mineral phosphoresces varies according to the mineral, and its intensity decreases over time.

Piezoelectricity: property of some minerals to produce a charge when under mechanical pressure. This is used in gas lighters, to produce sparks.

Plate tectonics: study of the formation and movement of the rigid pieces, or plates, that cover the Earth's surface.

Plutonic rock: an igneous rock that is formed when magma cools beneath the Earth's crust.

Granite is a plutonic rock.

Pyroelectricity: the property some minerals have of becoming electrically charged when heated or cooled.

Refraction: bending of light at the boundary between two substances — for example, as it passes from air to water. Each transparent or translucent substance bends light a characteristic amount, which is helpful in identifying unknown minerals. *See* Index of refraction.

Resin: sticky substance produced by certain plants (conifers). Amber is a fossil resin. Because it is sticky, many insects got trapped in the resin that later became amber, and they left an interesting fossil record.

Sandpaper: paper coated with sand according to the size of the glass powder particles.

Seam: a thin layer or stratum of rock between distinctive layers. This term is also used to describe the part of a mine tunnel being worked.

Sedimentary rocks: rocks formed from sediments bound together in some way. The sediments may consist of rock fragments, plant or animal remains, or chemicals; they form on lake and ocean bottoms. Shale, sandstone, rock salt, and limestone are sedimentary rocks.

Silicates: compounds of the elements silicon and oxygen. More than 90% of the minerals in the Earth's crust are silicates.

Stratification: the arrangement of sediment in overlapping layers (strata).

Streak: a mark made on an unglazed porcelain plate (streak plate), used as a means of identifying minerals. The color that appears (the mineral's inherent color) may be different than the color of the solid mineral. Minerals above hardness 6 must be ground up and rubbed across the plate. Softer minerals can be streaked across whole.

Strike: angle of a geologic layer in relation to the Earth's magnetic north, which can be determined by using a compass.

Syncline: a downfold in rock layers.

Topographical map: map representing the shape of a piece of land, including its naturally occurring features.

Twinning: joining of two or more crystals of the same mineral, according to the laws belonging to the symmetry of the crystal. These crystals can interpenetrate.

Ultraviolet light: A form of short-wavelength radiation located beyond the violet end of the spectrum; it is invisible to people.

Vein: a narrow layer of a minable mineral material.

Vitreous: having the brilliance and homogeneity of glass without having its transparency.

Wavelength: the distance between two successive wave crests.

Weathering: the process by which rocks are broken down, by the action of water, climate, and organisms.

INDEX